# MORE STUFF
## SELECTED LIVESEY PROJECTS 1973-2018

AF070268

Published by Applied Research and Design Publishing, an imprint of ORO Editions.
Gordon Goff: Publisher

www.appliedresearchanddesign.com
info@appliedresearchanddesign.com

More Stuff: Copyright © 2020, Knowlton School, The Ohio State University.

All rights reserved. No part of this book may be reproduced, stored in a retrieval system, or transmitted in any form or by any means, including electronic, mechanical, photocopying of microfilming, recording, or otherwise (except that copying permitted by Sections 107 and 108 of the U.S. Copyright Law and except by reviewers for the public press) without written permission from the publisher.

You must not circulate this book in any other binding or cover and you must impose this same condition on any acquirer.

Author: Robert Livesey
Editor: Benjamin Wilke
Book Design: Benjamin Wilke
Project Manager: Jake Anderson

10 9 8 7 6 5 4 3 2 1 First Edition

ISBN: 978-1-951541-03-3

Color Separations and Printing: ORO Group Ltd.
Printed in China.
Typeface: Akzidenz-Grotesk Pro

AR+D Publishing makes a continuous effort to minimize the overall carbon footprint of its publications. As part of this goal, AR+D, in association with Global ReLeaf, arranges to plant trees to replace those used in the manufacturing of the paper produced for its books. Global ReLeaf is an international campaign run by American Forests, one of the world's oldest nonprofit conservation organizations. Global ReLeaf is American Forests' education and action program that helps individuals, organizations, agencies, and corporations improve the local and global environment by planting and caring for trees.

# CONTENTS

| | |
|---|---|
| 4 | Introduction |
| 6 | Maison Truc |
| 12 | Solow Townhouses |
| 16 | Late Entry to the *Chicago Tribune* Competition |
| 18 | Baum Residence |
| 22 | Harold Nestor Hall, Columbus State Community College |
| 26 | Austrian Cultural Institute |
| 30 | Warren Street |
| 34 | Old Kings Highway |
| 38 | Town Street Condominiums |
| 42 | Northern Kentucky University Gateway |
| 46 | Fuzhou University Research Building |

# INTRODUCTION

*Architecture Stuff* is about looking at architecture; *More Stuff* is about making architecture. The same rules apply. The buildings that follow do not use the buildings discussed in *Architecture Stuff* as models. If anything, making buildings and developing ideas contributes to the way in which things are thought about and looked at in *Architecture Stuff*.

If one could say that the buildings seen in *Architecture Stuff* are eclectic and episodic, densely packed, acted upon, quote from the history of architecture and contemporary culture, have presence but lack hierarchy, are composed of elements and systems, iterate and conjugate, are both literal and abstract, absorb their context, are inventive, have amenities but are anti-consumerist, are humorous, and have unity and variety, then those buildings are not a bad introduction to what follows here. Surely, in those examples there is accommodation (program), economics (budget), and what we might call firmness (structure and weather resistance), but these elements alone are not what make architecture.

Stuff allows elements, space, and action to be generalized. Identifiable space becomes elemental. Actions have formal consequences. These are all things that can be juxtaposed, clustered, or manipulated. Informality allows for accessibility. Economy of gesture encourages more stuff and helps to establish density. Anomalies, incidents, and even accidents can occur. In all of this, there is a certain relentlessness. One can never give up and there is always more to do. An important aspect of architecture stuff is that it undercuts stasis. The idea that architecture is the result of having been acted upon means that what may seem fixed could have been moved. Of course, literal movement is also possible.

Architecture stuff is also irreverent. Play is important; Lucy the Margate Elephant has always been an inspiration. Architecture stuff is not afraid of the literal or the mundane. But, in its "urgent presentism," it is not dumb. Rather, its use of flat fact as symbol is an introduction to what William Jordy called "symbolic objectivity," and what he labeled as, "a mythic factuality omnipresent in modern experience … Its function is the comprehensiveness with which it brings disparate aspects of practical, aesthetic, psychic and metaphysical experience to focus in works of art."

As part of a language, elements of architecture stuff are defined in terms of one another. A diagrammatic understanding reveals latent organizations and relationships.

Plans and sections can also reveal these relationships. Le Corbusier said it best: "The plan is the generator. Without a plan, you have a lack of order and willfulness." The latter could be changed to: "With the plan, you have order and willfulness with which to make architecture stuff."

Being an unabashed formalist does not mean that one does not have societal concerns. It means that the language of architecture is, by its very nature, built form. Like the projects in *Architecture Stuff*, the buildings here are not an exhaustive collection but are purposely chosen as examples that demonstrate how stuff can calibrate and organize an architecture.

Lucy the Margate Elephant

# MAISON TRUC

Mt. Kisco, New York

Maison Truc is a reevaluation of the values of early 20th-century modernism in late 20th-century forms. Developed in 1973 while at the American Academy in Rome, the image of the truck recalls an earlier optimism for trains, boats, and planes. However, the utopian idealism of a former time comes to terms with the prevailing cultural disposition of *finding an easier way*. Technologically ordinary rather than new or outstanding, the truck admits to no ideal and is somewhat further understated by the fact that *truc* means "trinket" in French. Devoid of the serene glamour of the passenger ship or the airplane of the twenties, the truck is simply a pragmatic way to get something from here to there. As we perceive it on the open American road, the truck has inherent values that endow it with symbolic content.

In its most literal sense the truck is a representation of portable space that is cheaply mass-produced. Independence is its ideal and transience is its reality. Instead of a larger house with an emphasis on comfort, the spatial limits of the truck-box establish a smaller house with an emphasis on content (i.e., meaning). Removed from the ground, the trailers provide a volume that is equalized in three dimensions (with a 2'-6" module) in which artifacts supplant appliances and specified space replaces spatial largesse. It is all cowboy, this truck. The champagne and silver slippers of the twenties and the glories of the Castle Walk have been run over by the Marlboro Man.

Taking up little space but with more character, the functions of a house are reimagined as transient objects, and although some of the elements do have Pop connotations, they are not to be seen in isolation. Rather, they are part of an elaborate treasure hunt in which the trinkets are meant to give character to the elements of the house. Thus, the diesel exhaust vents the oven; the closet door rolls up; the study windows are abstracted truck graphics; the coffee table is a skid; the 7th Avenue pushcarts are clothes storage; and the trailer wheels describe an Ionic capital.

There is an occasional gesture toward the image of stately home. The ping-pong ball catcher is at once a cornice and a Baroque balustrade; the roof terrace handrail bulges to a Tuscan oil drop; and the projections on the street facade represent Renaissance balconies. But ultimately the notion of a house is not to be established by image, that is the vehicle for the truck. Rather, it is in opposition to that image as a truck-stop or as a continuation of the abstract cubist ideas of the twenties that the house is to achieve its character.

As a shield from the street, the truck-stop facade defers to the neighborhood context and allows for a distortion of image behind. Although the facade largely conceals the truck, the exposed cab confers the caprice of mobility on an otherwise stable object, thus implying that the conventional suburban house shelters an essentially transient society. Yet this image is no less applied than a conventional Colonial one, since the expression of transience is only symbolic; the truck does not actually move.

Because one's view of the truck cab through the driveway entrance foretells of a private world cloaked with respectability by the street facade, it introduces a larger effort to comment on suburban access and privacy. Juxtaposed with the public frontality of the truckstop facade directed toward the neighborhood, the private frontality of the driveway facade (the cab and the trailers) can be inferred from the A-B-A modulation of the Renaissance palazzo organization of the street facade. The cab and trailers form their own truck-house facade that contains the real (or everyday) entrance between the two trailers.

Inserted in the public facade at the street door, an unusually high sill interrupts the processional entrance by making it a struggle to get through, thereby physically demonstrating that this entrance is a merely a representation of entrance. Besides its obvious statement about suburbia, this gesture is also an introduction to a series of events that attempt to make explicit and accessible some primary architectural notions of procession, alternate route, and urbanism. By removing the entrance function from the processional entrance, the genuflection sill attempts to point out the organizational potential of an entrance. The fire pole, slide, ladder, and stairs irreverently reveal the possibilities of alternate route. The subway grating, alleyway, loading shaft, and areaway imply an urbanism that—besides its contradiction of contexts—refers to a layering or density of experience.

Having established density of meaning as a virtue, there are other elaborations that establish an architecture of stuff. Continuing with the elements themselves, a layering is further developed in the double reading of the void of the street facade at the driveway. The facade has been both cut away, as represented by the drive-in movie screen (which also marks the potential growth of the scheme at three trailers), and pulled apart, as allowed by the fixed structure of the catwalk operating as a track for the sliding wall. This duality oscillating as it does between one reading and the other is a portrayal of ambiguity and as such is in contrast with the specific definitions assigned to the compressed and crushed corners. They are defined by a revealed interior and a bulging darkroom wall in the first case and by an inverted corner and consistency of material in the second.

However, no matter how developed the objects become, one cannot claim architecture stuff without conquering space. But precisely because space is the sine qua non

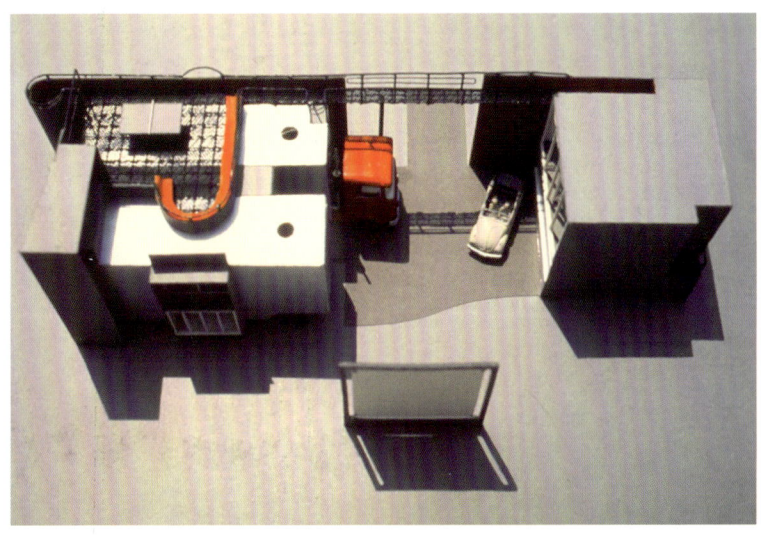

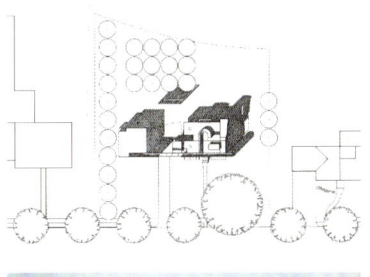

of architecture, once this has been achieved, one will have to admit that architecture has been transformed and further that the reduction of space to a trinket has the possibility of freeing architecture of its spatial bias. As the objects assumed a preference for strongly differentiated meaning over squandered image, perhaps space can become a familiar elemental character by a particular distortion of volume. Thus, the kitchen and study are characterized not by their size or content (which are essentially the same) in that the appliances and furniture have been equated as artifacts, but by the distortions (contractions and extensions) of the spaces. The kitchen is bordered on three sides by a glass projection to the street, the gallery of the upper hall, and the yellow horizontal "sunset" tube of the diesel exhaust above the stove, while the study is relieved only at its circular skylight and constricted slits.

As a continuation of the idea of specified space, the living room no longer achieves its specificity by content, but by more distinct distortions of the volume. The oil drum, the narrowing of the hall, the landing at the bottom of the study steps, the balcony and its relocated space on the garden facade, and the extension of the dining room sideboard all act to give the space a specific configuration that can be recognized and identified. On the one hand, this thing is no longer a space. It is a leftover and simply a consequence of the actions upon it. On the other hand, as these actions can be perceived and understood, they make this thing more than a space. It is a trinket that can be carried around in a pocket of the mind: a favorite button that can be examined again and again.

Having established an architecture made of stuff, the studio-garage exists as a remembrance from which it all comes. The fragments of truck siding on the darkroom wall and the garage door, the piece of kitchen, the sheetrock wall, and the guest couch are part of a cubist composition and exist in contrast to the more complete images of the neo-cubist truck-house. The space of the truck-box is also generalized in its three dimensions, whereas the space of the studio-garage sits on the ground and again is fragmented.

Maison Truc is a reflection of its time and is at once a comment on contemporary society, urbanism, suburban living, and the then-current architectural obsessions. It is the beginning of an equation that accounts for artifacts and actions in an attempt to add character to architecture stuff.

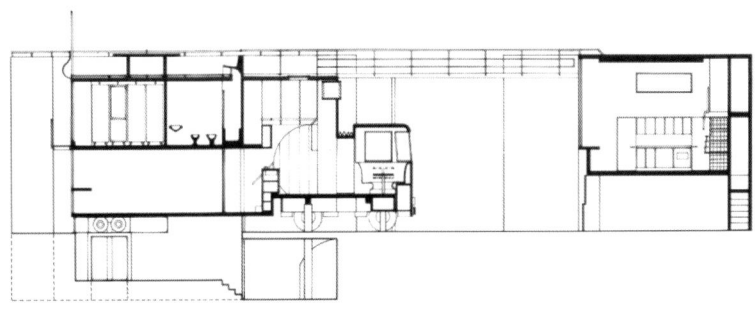

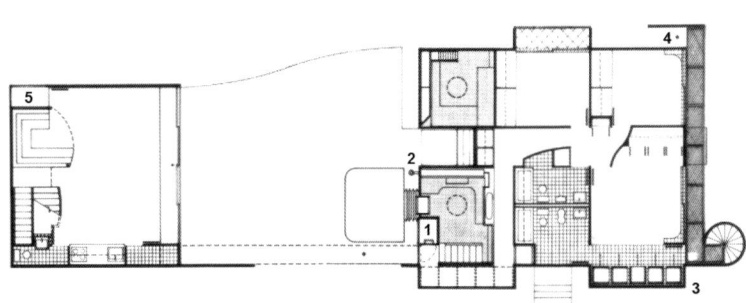

**SECOND FLOOR**
1 CRUSHED CORNER  2 DIESEL EXHAUST  3 7TH AVENUE STORAGE  4 FIRE POLE  5 COMPRESSED CORNER

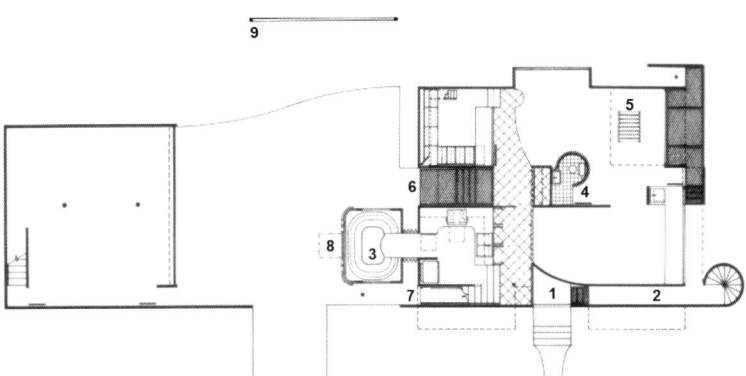

**FIRST FLOOR**
1 GENUFLECTION SILL  2 ALLEYWAY  3 HYDRAULIC TABLE  4 OIL DRUM W.C.  5 SKID
6 SUBWAY GRADING  7 SLIDE  8 PROJECTION BOOTH  9 PROJECTION SCREEN

# SOLOW TOWNHOUSES
with James Stirling

New York, New York

The Solow Townhouses are a proposal for a limited design competition between Richard Meier and James Stirling for the developer Sheldon Solow in 1978. Our entry proposes townhouses to be built over an underground two-story parking garage adjacent to a 40-story Miesian glass residential tower at 2nd Avenue and 62nd Street in New York City. The structure of the townhouses needs to approximate the 18-foot bays of the garage. The three different unit types are to be luxury housing with large entertaining spaces and amenities such as private elevators. Stirling wanted to emulate the idiosyncratic character of the Upper East Side townhouses. The varying widths of the units reflected the then-physique of the designers. What developed are fat and thin elements that provide a unique rhythm to the row. By pulling the elevator and stair out of the thin units, every residence has an 18' x 36' living room.

Within the units, the served spaces are objectified by being emphatically-shaped. The service spaces are carved from the resultant poche. Roof lights provide light to the stairs and top-floor studies. The lower unit in the fat townhouse has a kitchen, dining room, and garden room facing the back garden. A maid's room faces the street. The living room is on the piano nobile with four bedrooms on the third floor. The maisonette above has an entry hall, maid's room, and elevator on the ground floor. The bedrooms are on the fourth floor, while the living room, dining room, and libraries are on the fifth floor, accessible by an elevator. There is a garden room on the roof. The thin units are more traditional townhouse layouts, with a maid's room and garden room on the ground floor, kitchen and dining room on the second floor, living room and study on the third floor, and two bedrooms on each of the fourth and fifth floors.

On the street elevation, bow windows, artist studio windows, balconies, and gardens help to articulate differences between the units and give the units character and identity. The thin units are projected and sheared with an overscaled and voided keystone. The recessed wide units are more figural, with rusticated bases, bow windows, and artist studio windows on top. Thus, *fat* and *thin* are not simply descriptive of the massing or building elements, they also operate as both representational and abstract.

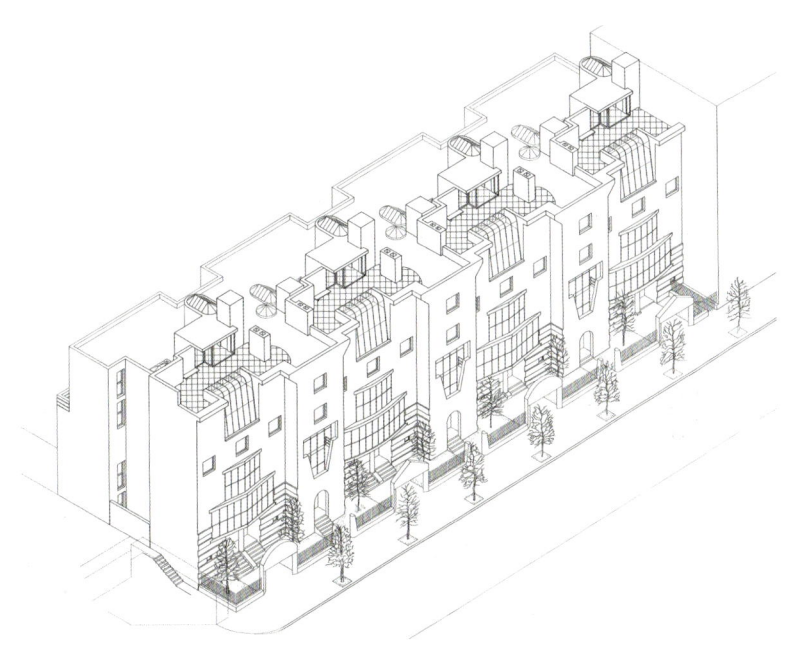

FLOOR 4  FLOOR 5

FLOOR 2  FLOOR 3

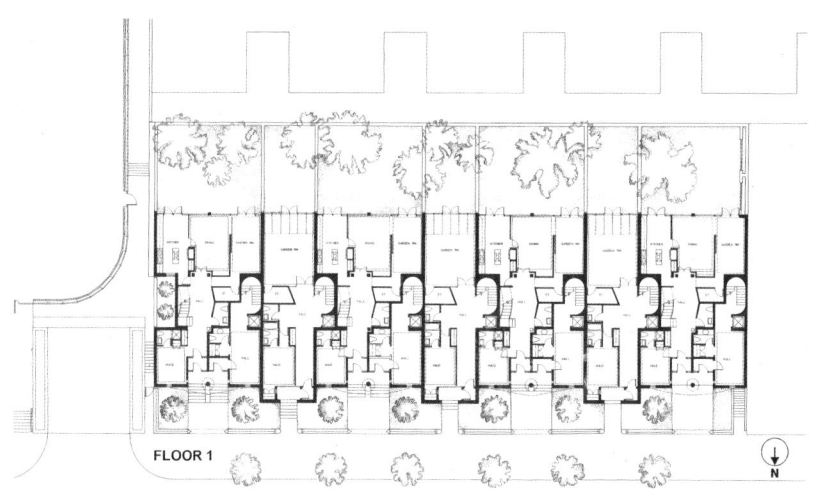

FLOOR 1

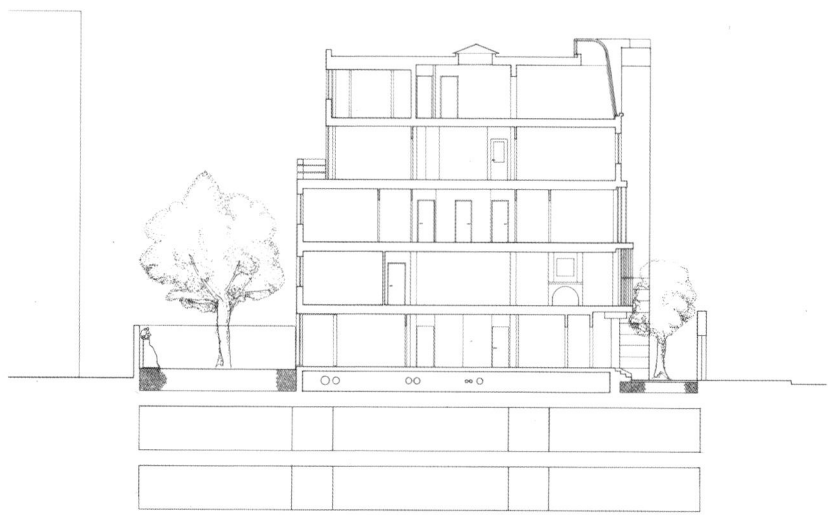

# LATE ENTRY TO THE CHICAGO TRIBUNE COMPETITION
with Turan Duda

Chicago, Illinois

In 1922, the *Chicago Tribune* held a design competition for its new headquarters. Entries arrived from all over the world. The prize money for 2nd place allowed Eliel Saarinen (father of Eero) to immigrate to the United States. Among the iconic entries was Adolph Loos's Doric column sitting on a block base. In 1967, Claus Oldenberg submitted a late entry to the *Chicago Tribune* Competition.

In 1980, Stanley Tigerman organized an exhibition called "Late Entries to the *Chicago Tribune* Tower Competition" and invited 100 architects to participate. The rules allowed for a single image of the canonic view. Our entry celebrated Loos's entry to the original competition, acknowledged the popular imagery of the Oldenberg entry, and called out the infantile humor emanating from Chicago at the time, as Tigerman had just published the "Daisy House."

In our proposal, the block base accommodates the *Chicago Tribune* printing presses, the bottle houses the editorial offices, the cap is a revolving restaurant, and the nipple contains the mechanical equipment.

Loos's entry

Oldenberg's entry

LATE ENTRY TO THE CHICAGO TRIBUNE COMPETITION

# BAUM RESIDENCE
with Mark Rosenstein

Fairfield Beach, Connecticut

Designed in 1982, the proposal for the Baum House is located on the only double-wide lot on a 200-foot-deep spit of land facing the Long Island Sound. The residence is designed for a retired couple who wanted to sell their suburban home and move to the beach full time. The clients also wanted to accommodate the families of their grown children and allow their friends to use their beach without entering the house.

The street elevation references both the grandeur of the Low House by McKim, Mead & White, and the Baum's former suburban residence. The facade elements are shifted, but ultimately subservient to the taut skin and punched-up gable of the elevation. Located on a ridge that separates the bay from the sound, the house is raised an additional 30 inches to allow the water to pass underneath in the event of a hurricane. The recessed vestibule facade is a knock-out panel and the public entrance to the house. The sea portal invites family and friends through the screen porch to the water.

The beach elevation emulates the scale of the tacky, adjacent beach houses, with architectural elements that have been washed ashore from near and far. The potter's shed (that functions as the changing rooms) come from a larger estate down the coast. The screen porch is the temple of Poseidon washed in from Sounion, Greece. The two-story porch is from the Georgia coast. The tower is a lighthouse beckoning to its sibling in the water. The continuity of the wall of architectural bits allows the facade to read as flapping in the breeze. The wooden deck is both an idealized beach and a tray to hold the beached debris.

The house allows for both the informality of the beach and the formality of the couple. As one moves through the house, the stately home is transformed into a discombobulated beachfront. In plan, short axes and symmetry are broken and deformed. The architectural allusions continue in a formal front hall, an Empire dining room, a gallery living room, a master bedroom sound lock (to quiet the din of the grandchildren), and a Louis XIV master bed alcove. The references become more playful with a fried egg linoleum floor in the kitchen, a soap bubble floor in the laundry, a jacuzzi with a view, and a lookout that is only accessible by an elevator.

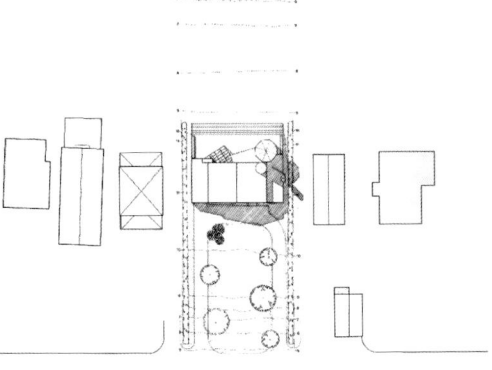

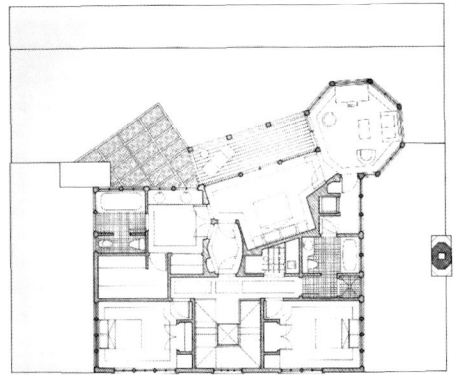

**SECOND FLOOR**

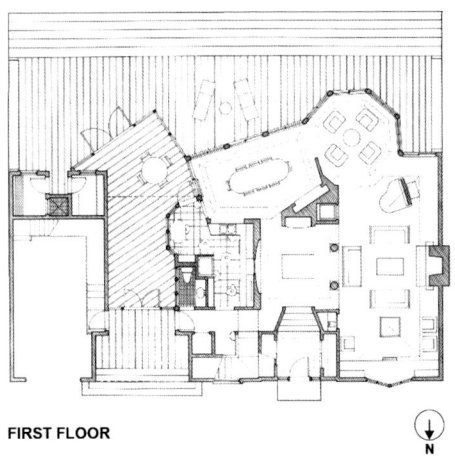

**FIRST FLOOR**

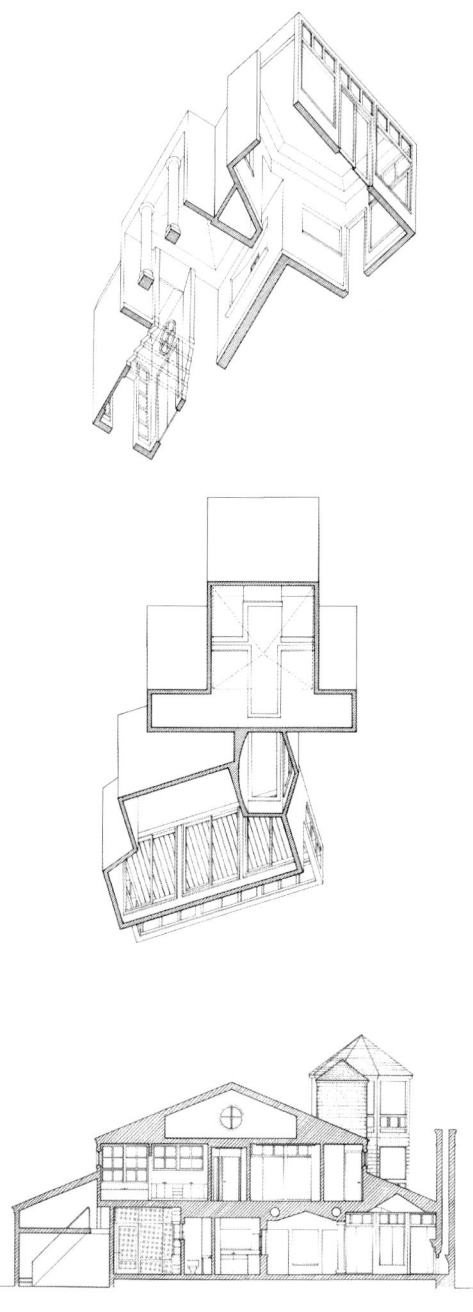

# HAROLD NESTOR HALL
with NBBJ

Columbus, Ohio

Designed in 1991, Harold Nestor Hall is a b(a)roque ensemble of numerical, material, architectural, and programmatic elements. The building is a 127,000-square-foot facility for a community college that attempts to resolve the conflicting energies bearing on an urban academic center without taming them into genteel submission. Because the existing campus is indicative of a somewhat deadpan '60s architecture, Nestor Hall cannot exactly fit in.

The best part of the campus is its original quadrangle. Nestor Hall forms another courtyard at the end of the vestigial administrative axis and marks it with a student lounge that juxtaposes students and administration while elaborating both the organizational and nascent attributes of the campus. This game is played out in multiple center and edge reversals and in the expansion of the material palette. The result is a building that is comfortable in its context but in no way limited by it.

As a classroom building with student lounges, a performance theater, a conference center, and faculty offices, the building is a center of campus and a gateway between "town and gown." Normally one would think of a classroom building as a "background" building. However, the college is at the edge of town and needs to establish a stronger identity in its location. Relatively long and skinny, the building allows for more light into the classrooms while creating more presence on the site.

The curve of the building allows it to align with the local road configuration and more directly face the downtown; it is a bit of American urbanism by being both infill and object. It is a city wall that pushes back sprawl while serving as an announcement or billboard for the community college. The facade on the town side is formal and stately enough to allow the community college to be properly presented to the local business community; the facade on the campus side is much more playful in order to clearly identify this building as a place for the students.

The massing of the building is a non-ideal curve that sutures the campus grain to the urban context. The order of the form is constantly changing: the building is at once 10, 12, and 14 bays. On the south elevation, the louvers, arches, and windows each march to a different rhythm. The diagonal pattern of the brick studs stitches the windows together. The structural bay is six modules, but the room pattern is four. When the systems align, they mark an event.

The sculpted elevator shafts, arches, theater mass, rotated ramp, and bulging glass express the myriad forces operating within the building. The windows—emblematic of the elaboration of architectural elements—are choreographed in various ways: sometimes carefully proportioned, quadrupled, quartered, gridded, stripped, de-mullioned, punched, bent, and finally laid to rest. The building is most easily summed up as a collision of systems where each system carries importance but no system is allowed to dominate. The multiple centers of the gateway, building configuration, and elevator towers are examples of the interactive systems that provide a different reading of the building with each experience.

The primary material for the exterior wall is the beige iron-spot brick found elsewhere on campus. Here it is studded with red brick accents on the south elevation, and elsewhere augmented with patterned red brick, polished granite, and spotted corrugated metal.

As a multi-purpose facility, this is a building with many masters. It serves each with a rich palette of materials and architectural elements, some as simple as the waiting arcade or the sitting wall. Some elements are more complex, like the break space for the conference center on the lower level that intersects with the student lounge above and throws the view of campus out of kilter. All pieces are part of a larger puzzle and play multiple roles in establishing the building as a center for the campus and a gateway to a new world.

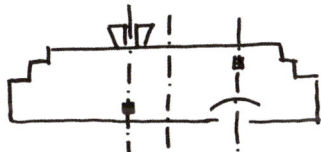

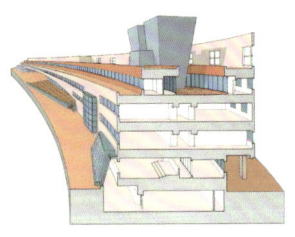
TRANSVERSE SECTION
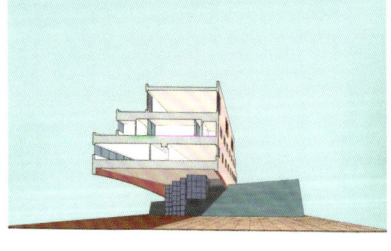
GATEWAY SECTION

24  MORE STUFF

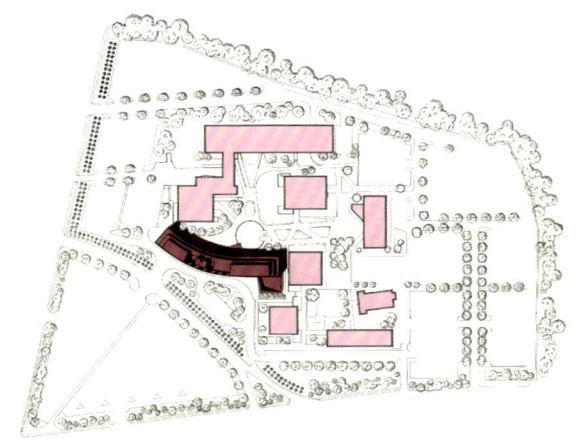

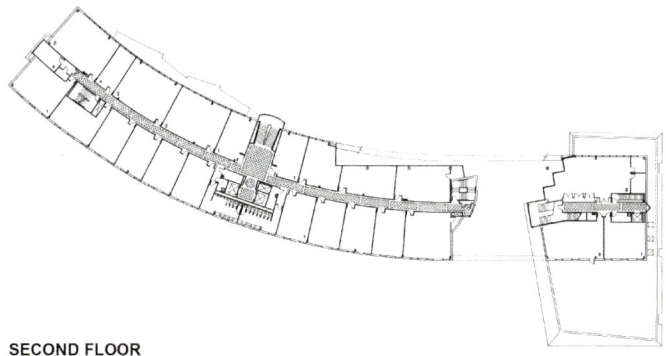

**SECOND FLOOR**

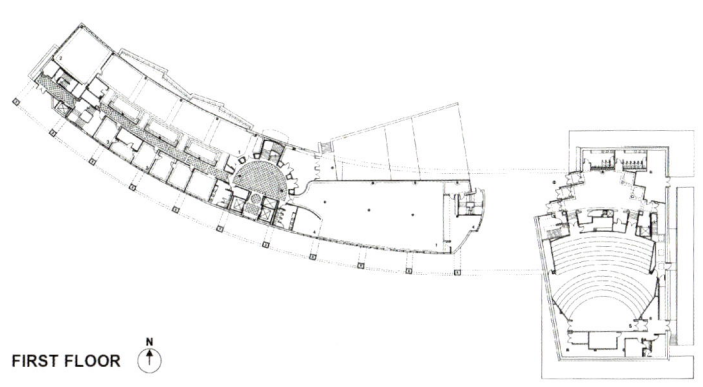

**FIRST FLOOR** N ↑

# AUSTRIAN CULTURAL INSTITUTE
with Friedl Bohm and Jeffrey Kipnis

New York, New York

The Austrian Cultural Institute (now called the Austrian Cultural Forum) in New York City is a competition entry from 1992. The proposal is a collage of Austrian culture, synthesized with Manhattan's glass skyscraper tradition to make a frank and contemporary building. An ambitious program dictates that the zoning box be filled, resulting in a sliver tower. Small but highly articulate in comparison to its large-scale neighbors, the building seems appropriate for a representation of Austria in the USA.

Visitors are introduced to the Institute by virtue of an architectural rendering of the Austrian flag that hangs as a banner on East 52nd Street. The flag, a projected box materialized in red colored glass and alabaster (each of which is backlit at night), establishes a clear symbolic presence and imparts a contextual transition between its neighbors, a large concrete frame skyscraper and a lower, bulkier, masonry hotel. The flag also acts to articulate a cultural threshold between New York on the outside and Austria on the inside.

Leaving New York, visitors enter a Viennese lobby influenced by the interiors of the seminal Austrian architect Adolf Loos. A grand staircase takes visitors up and down to the two largest public spaces: the multipurpose room and the exhibition gallery. Both spaces continue a recall of Austrian heritage. The gallery floor is given a two-dimensional pattern reminiscent of the country's jagged mountains and non-orthogonal architectural investigations. The multipurpose room's form emulates a baroque opera house while its perforated metal surface evokes contemporary Austrian architectural material experimentation. Further up in the building, the video theater is the reverse. Made of traditional materials, the form resonates with Austria's renowned architectural avant-garde. The library, recalling the academy, and the director's penthouse as a belvedere continue the theme of inserting Austrian elements in the middle of Manhattan. Offices and temporary accommodations are interspersed and become the rock formations that make up the mountain.

The Austrian collage introduced by the flag and continued on the interior is brought to conclusion in the massing of the blue-glass shard. Drawing upon the heritage of the Austrian Baroque and the picturesque forms of the Austrian Alps, a complex, non-orthogonal geometry inflects the traditional glass box to form a unique and irreducible three-dimensional architectural form. The synthesis ensures that the project is both a representation of Austria and a building that is recognizable in its architectural setting.

AUSTRIAN CULTURAL INSTITUTE

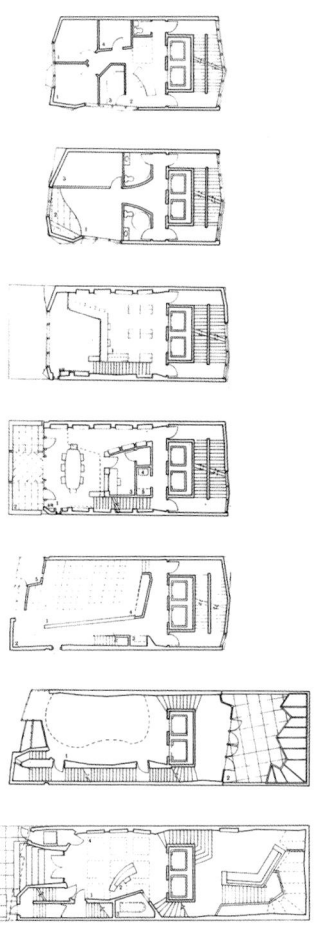
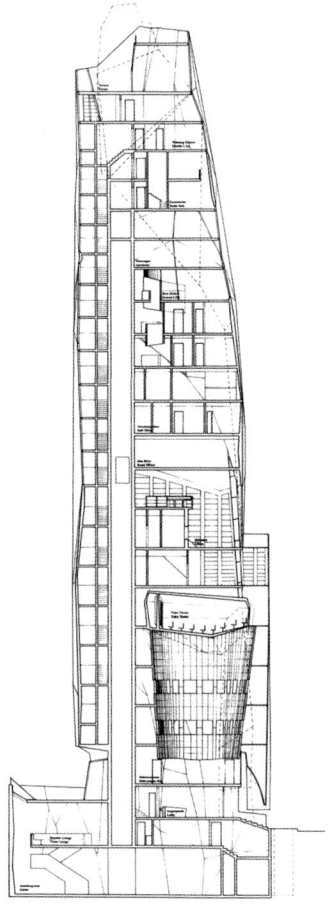

28  MORE STUFF

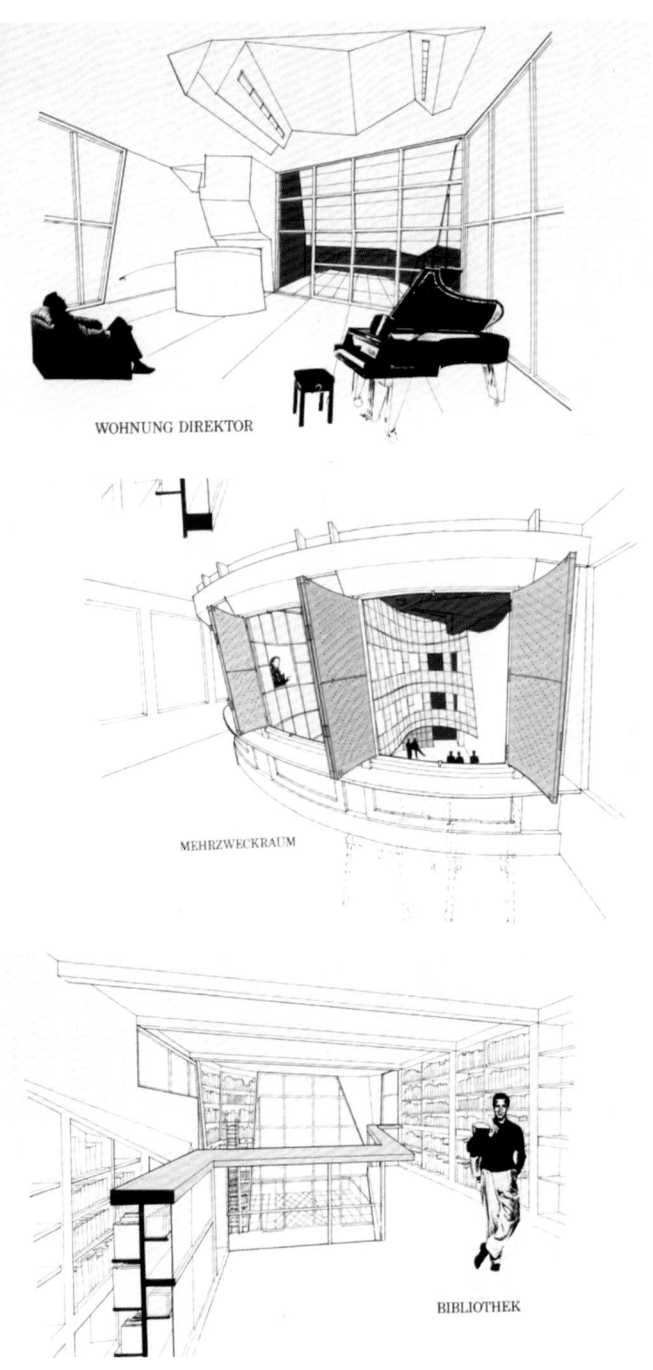

WOHNUNG DIREKTOR

MEHRZWECKRAUM

BIBLIOTHEK

# WARREN STREET

Columbus, Ohio

58 Warren Street is an addition and renovation in a near-in neighborhood in Columbus, Ohio. The original house was built in 1895 as a typical Italianate worker's house: a "two-up, two-down" with a single-story gabled kitchen wing in the back. The neighborhood contains a mixture of commercial and residential buildings where Italianate and Queen Anne styles predominate. Completed in 1999, Warren Street absorbs the context by purifying the existing house and adding a contemporary "Queen Anne equivalent" garage-studio.

The old and new elements are stapled together by a corrugated metal stair tower. The metal reflects the area's rich mixture of commercial types and is a remembrance of an old manufacturing building that used to occupy the adjacent lot. Mixing masonry and wood with metal is not easy; all three materials are affected by being pinched, pushed, ripped, and compressed. The results register on the surfaces.

The massing of the adjoining two-family house is mirrored in the garden elevation of the studio wing that is pulled back on the second floor to allow the morning sun to sweep the back lawn. The siding is "signboard," with the battens suggesting the scale of the stone on the adjacent house. Contrasting with the brick, the siding further distinguishes the Queen Anne from the Italianate. The kitchen wing becomes the garden pavilion and is objectified by the reveal of the metal stair.

In the addition, the glass garage doors relate to the horizontal void of a porch across the street and recall the auto repair shops that used to dot the neighborhood. The doors allow for a view from the street to the back garden and turn the garage into a *porte-cochere* entrance for the house. When not inhabited by cars, the garage doubles as a party room. The frontcourt is public and open to the city. The back garden is a semi-private courtyard overlooked by the neighbors. The roof terrace is private with a view of downtown.

The first floor of the old house has been gutted to allow for loft living. The powder room wall is curved as part of the compression that occurred when the stair was jammed into the side of the kitchen wing. In the kitchen, the banquette creates a diner. The route to the second floor is a constructed Escher drawing. Upstairs, the stair tower is pushed into the bathroom and study, causing walls to bend and break and the handrail to fracture. The corner window of the studio overlaps with the stair hall and becomes a compressed conservatory. All parts are off-the-shelf, cheap, and readily accessible.

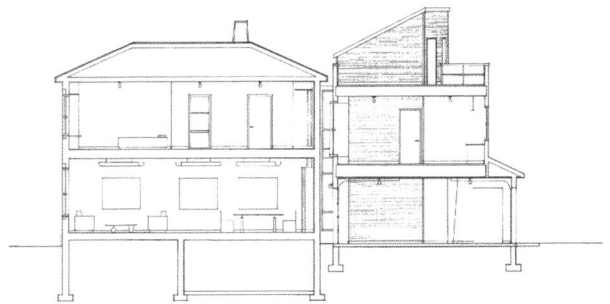

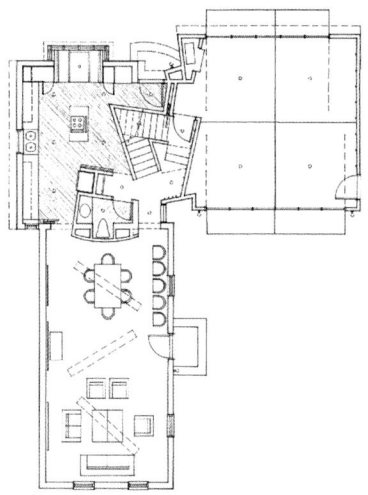

**SECOND FLOOR**

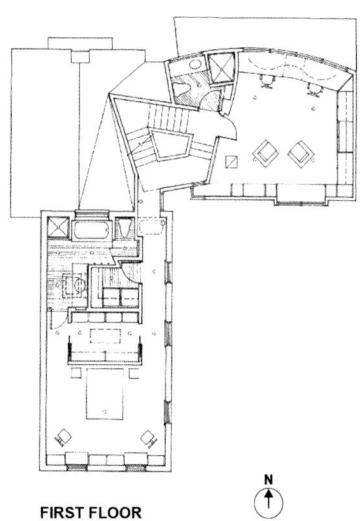

**FIRST FLOOR**

N

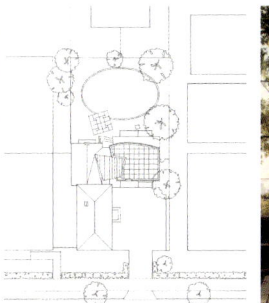

# OLD KINGS HIGHWAY

Weston, Connecticut

Designed in 2002, this five bedroom, 4½ bath house is not small. But at less than 4,000 square feet, it can accommodate a multi-generational family and is compartmentalized to allow for contracted and expanded living. Built on the foundations of a summer cottage, much of the accommodation is under an encompassing roof to reduce the house's mass. However, like all old New England homes, there are additions.

What the house lacks in mass it makes up in allusions ... or maybe illusions. From the Tudor stacked window to the battered (vine) ramparts, from the baroque balustrade to the carousel dining nook, from the overscaled Romani cart to the truck dormer, from the real chimney to its glass equivalent, and from the New England clapboard siding to the modernist glass wall, all of the elements are recognizable and make up a much more varied set of references than one might normally find in the suburbs.

Recognition is followed by elaboration. Windows, porches, stairs, rooms, recesses, and projections have multiple incarnations, with each providing a different understanding of the architectural element. Windows are not just big and small, compressed and scattered, graphic and sculpted, recessed and projected, punched, or stripped; they are folded around corners and recessed into the facade to illustrate volume and wall as different organizational systems.

Porches are equally elaborate and articulate. The formal front porch is recessed with a door and side window. The service porch is of a similar size, but projected with peephole and a door. The side garden entrance is again recessed, but this time with a Pope's balcony above. The garden deck off the living and dining rooms is both raised ground and a spit that juts into the garden. The balcony off the master bedroom is iron strapping removed from the Romani caravan and shades the glass wall of the dining room. On the third floor, the family can choose between a shaded breakfast balcony and a private sunning deck.

The stair hall to the attic, the ultra-thin back stair, and the deck's "Z" and straight stairs again elaborate differences within an element. It is not just the elements that register differences, actions are also recorded on the house. The bow window of the second-floor bedroom and third-floor balcony indicates a front-to-back compression. The extended front facade by the study indicates that the side of the house has been compressed. The facade jog by the dining room and master bedroom confirms these actions.

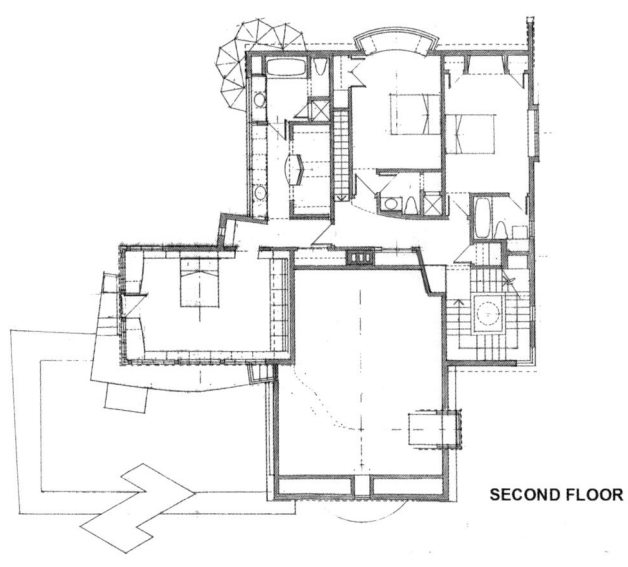

**SECOND FLOOR**

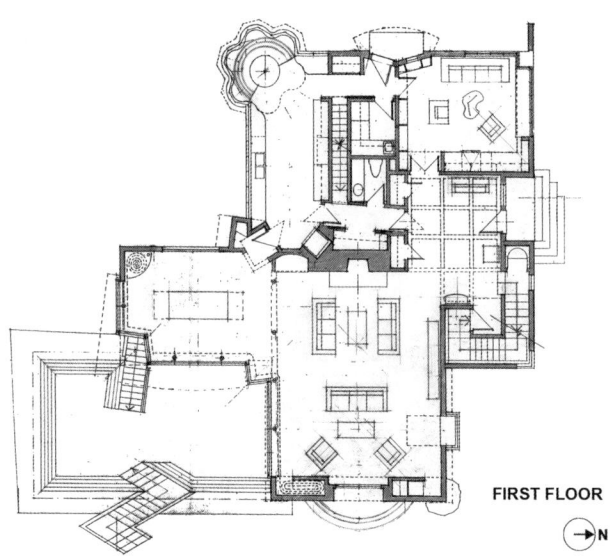

**FIRST FLOOR**

N

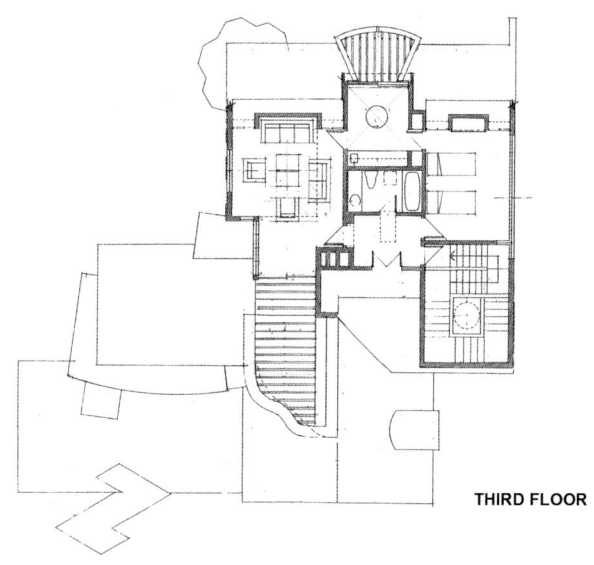

**THIRD FLOOR**

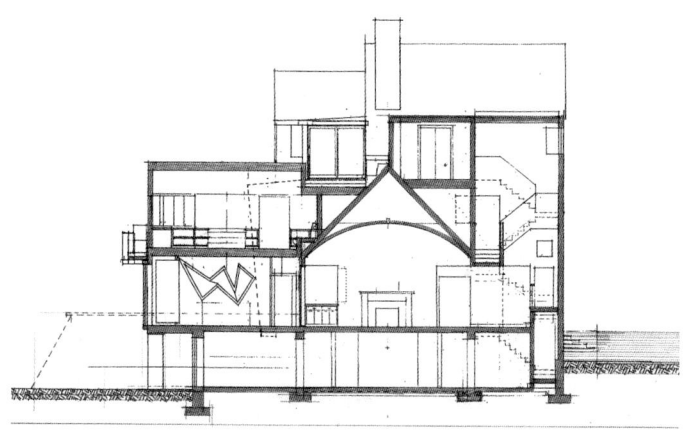

# TOWN STREET CONDOMINIUMS

Columbus, Ohio

Town Street Condominiums is a speculative project for a developer designed in 2006. With plenty of housing stock in near-in neighborhoods and few downtown amenities, it is not easy to encourage living in downtown Columbus, Ohio. Therefore, this design has to provide a critical mass, 120 units, and plenty of amenities. The residents are pampered with easy parking, a doorman, a concierge, a restaurant, a gallery, a health club, a pool, and a putting green. Twenty-five percent of the units have roof gardens.

The 40-foot cubic module mimics the scale of the stately homes (now converted into offices) that line the street. In the horizontal dimension, 40 feet and multiple exposures provide every space with natural light and air. In the vertical dimension, 40 feet allows for a generous three-and-a-half floors. At the roof, the half-floor accommodates depth for soil in the roof garden and a handrail. At the base, the half-floor raises the unit above the street for privacy. The building has two types of tops (half and full floors) as the modules flip on one and another.

The cubes are collected in I's, L's, Z's, and T's to form neighborhoods and add grandeur to the complex. The crescent and circus of Bath and the blocks of Regents Park are the models here, although here the forms are superimposed and indicative of a less gentile existence. A change of material and differentiation of color add a playful character to the elements. The skin is applied to the volumes and is abstract, as the letterforms are both horizontal and vertical. Although the letterforms are easily read, the double height sections in the units, event anomalies, and a fine grain circulation system provide other organizational structures for the complex.

The limited frontage on Town Street is the address to have. However, the complex also spans the alley to the back nine. From the entrance court to the putting green to the pool deck to the private roof gardens, one is never far removed from the outside or the views of downtown. The drop off court is sheltered and urban. The putting green is open and suburban. The sky pool deck is sunny and ephemeral. Residences vary from town homes on the street to tower lofts above. Choice is an amenity.

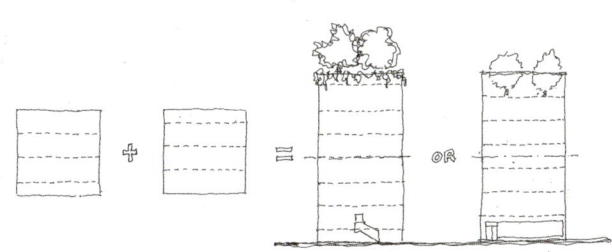

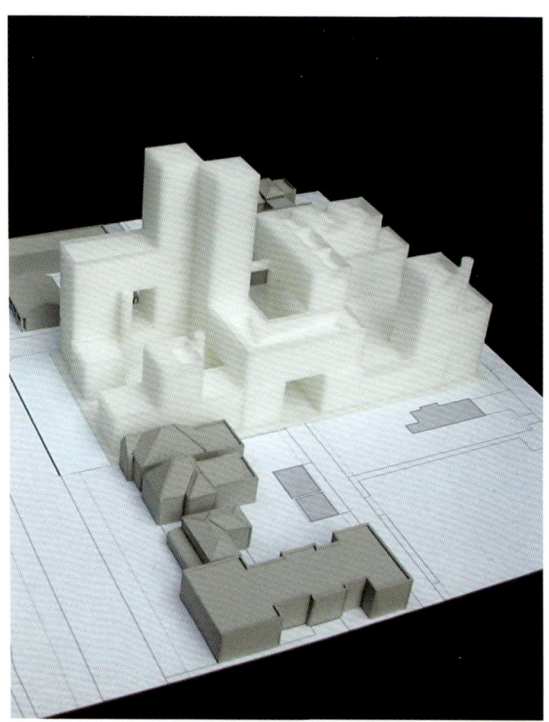
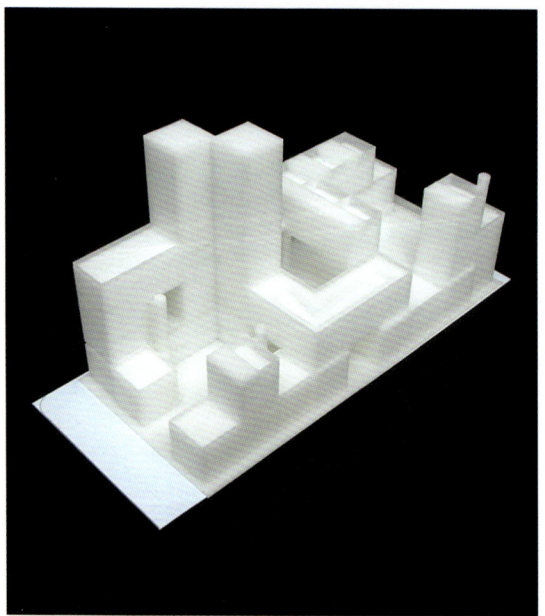

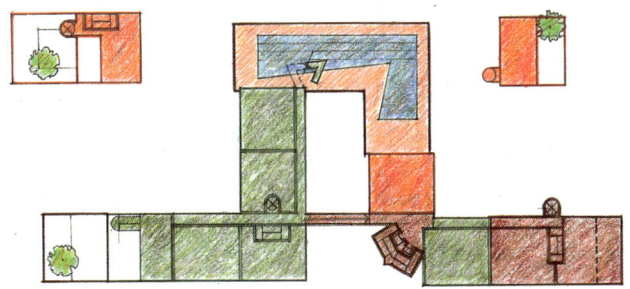

**SEVENTH FLOOR**

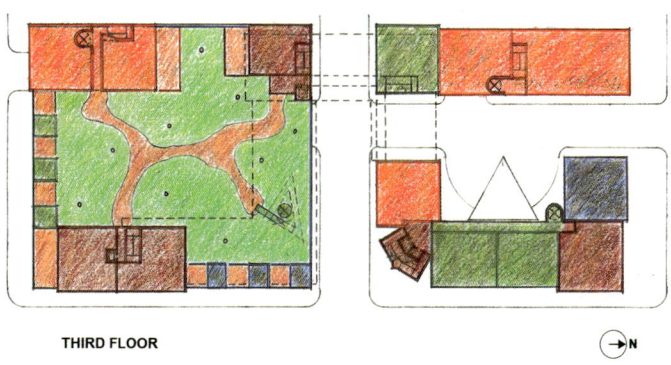

**THIRD FLOOR**

N

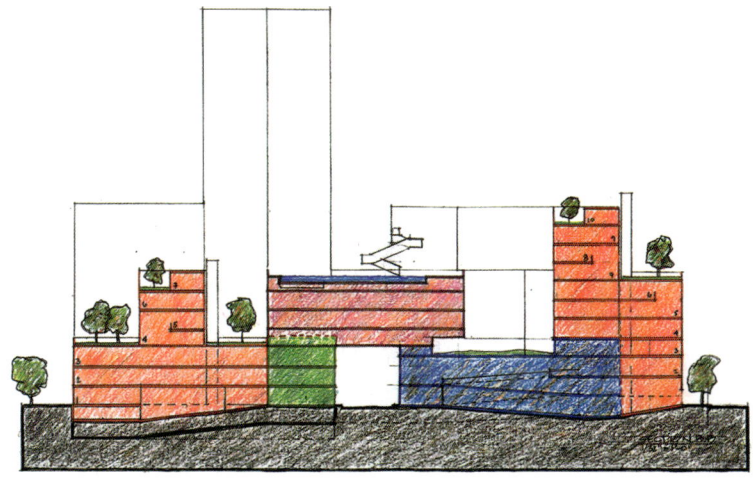

TOWN STREET CONDOMINIUMS

# NORTHERN KENTUCKY UNIVERSITY GATEWAY
with Moody Nolan

Highland Heights, Kentucky

Northern Kentucky University Gateway is the winning entry from a limited design competition in 2008. The project is located at the entrance to the campus, establishing a gateway and incentivizing partnerships with local industry. The site drops 45 feet along its length and has two utility right-of-ways that cross it. The program for the site is 420,000 square feet of commercial and retail space, a 100-room hotel, and parking for 1,200 cars. The right-of-ways help to separate the buildings for light, air, and phasing. The change in elevation allows for the close proximity of the buildings and encourages walkability. The pedestrian path in the middle of the site allows access to the buildings and underground parking.

The upper plaza is the face of the university in the town. The plaza is raised slightly to provide more presence while allowing parking underneath. The "life saver" skylights are the floral disc for the daisy paving and provide light to the parking below. A hotel faces both the street and the plaza. The retail and commercial building is set back and presents a facade for the rest of the development beyond. The project aligns the university entrance road with a "research" facade while the right-of-ways and other pedestrian paths connect to the adjacent residential neighborhood. The curb of the city street is indented to accommodate a bus stop. The daisy courtyards and their glass walls allow for respite along the pedestrian path as well as entrances to the buildings and parking. The lower (university) plaza is comparable in size to the upper (town) plaza and is bounded by Student Services and retail space.

Except for the green wall of the Student Services Building, the building skins are a mix of metal panels and glass. Although the buildings step down a hill, codes limit them to three stories each. Therefore, their massing is similar while their window configurations vary by using curvy horizontal windows, striaght vertical windows, and wonky punched windows. Except for the green wall, the scale of the floors within is hidden.

The project is phased, starting with the two ends—town and gown—and then filling the middle. In the interim, the undeveloped land functions as a tree farm for the university. The project is both an ensemble and a collection of discrete elements that work to pack the site.

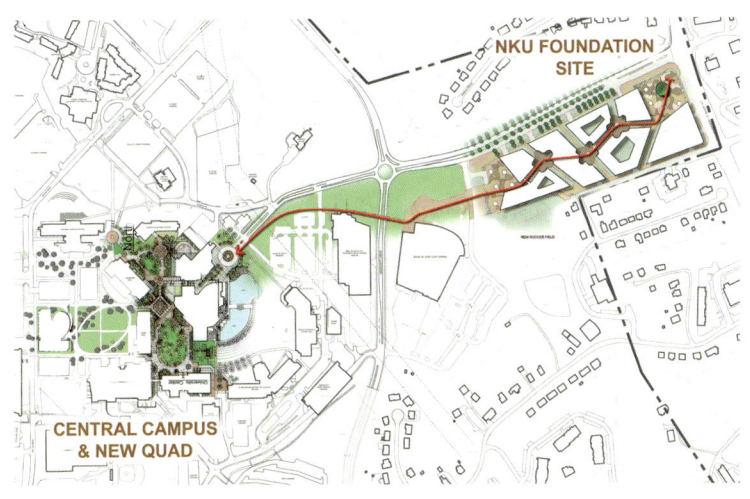

# FUZHOU UNIVERSITY RESEARCH BUILDING
with Yuhang Kong

Fuzhou, China

Designed in 2018, the Research Building at Fuzhou University in Southeast China is actually a redesign. The master plan for the campus was previously done and established limits for each new building on campus. Working within those limits, the 50,000-square-meter research building accommodates multiple organizations that use the talents of the University's faculty and students in the corporations' research. The two main requirements of the project are to provide light and air for the employees and to encourage interaction between the various constituents.

The newly-enhanced entrance to the campus from the north is down a monumental avenue that leads to a ring road. The project site is at the southwest corner of the campus with the primary entrance facing an extension of the ring road. Sitting on top of an underground parking garage, the structure of the building needs to align with the square bays of the parking level below. The three "pavilion" buildings are six bays wide and three bays deep; they are connected by single-bay bridges and bracketed by tapered side wings.

Two courtyards face south: one is contained while the other encourages a diagonal pass through the site. A central courtyard faces north: its three freestanding mounds and mounded edges are a center of activity.

In the pavilions, the center bay accommodates both vertical circulation and multiple-story spaces to encourage interaction between floors. The ground floor accommodates multiple entrances, three interconnected courtyards, two restaurants, and a large multipurpose room. On the upper floors, shared rest spaces are sprinkled throughout the building and are varied in size, shape, and scale. Some are single-story and some are multi-story. Some are centralized while some are at the edge. Some have balconies and others are adjacent to terraces. All of the rest areas are expressed on the elevations with cuts in the expanded metal screens that otherwise provide privacy and shade for the office windows. These rest areas are meant to attract corporations and workers to what is otherwise programmed as a generic office building; no workspace is more than a hundred steps from rest, relaxation, or access to exterior space.

The canted roofs give the building a presence on the skyline. The cuts in the roofs allow light and air deep into the building while making the intertwining volumetric spaces within the pavilions legible. The exposed stair towers continue a theme of similarity and difference. The stair in the southwest courtyard is next to an entrance and matches the standard cores while connecting the multipurpose room to the rest of the building. The core in the north courtyard is disconnected from the building at the ground and contains a fire elevator and stair. The core in the southeast court is all stair—providing escape in the event of a fire—but only going to the roof of the lower east wing.

Accommodating over 2,000 people, this is not a small building. With the pavilions and wings, and their respective courtyards, roof gardens, terraces, and balconies, the workers are never far from nature. In the end, a program that tends to result in monotonous or repetitive spaces here becomes a series of spaces that are individually recognizable and provide access to nature, light, and air.

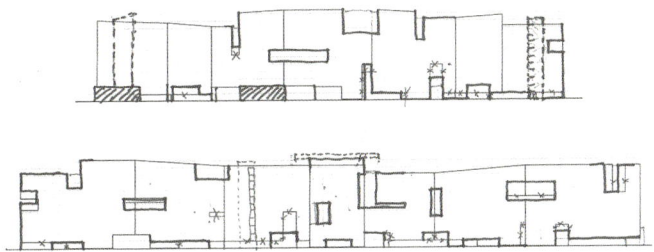

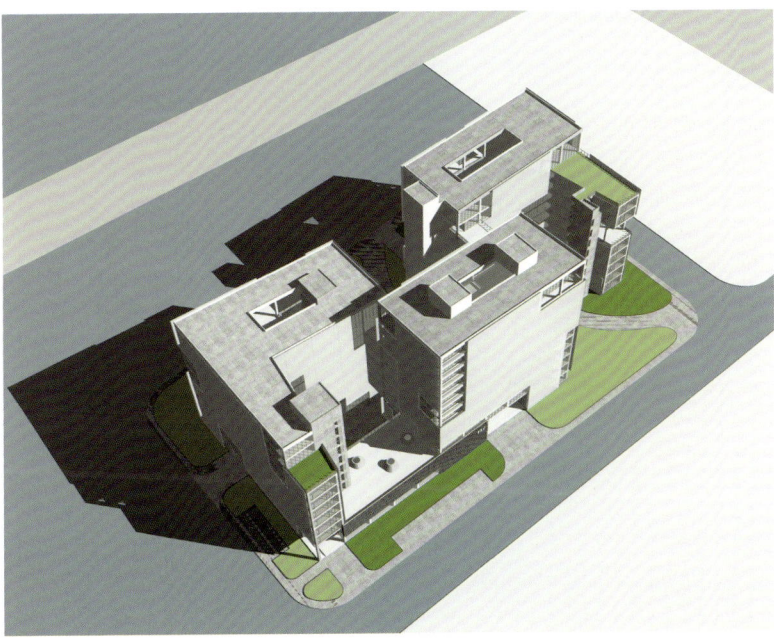

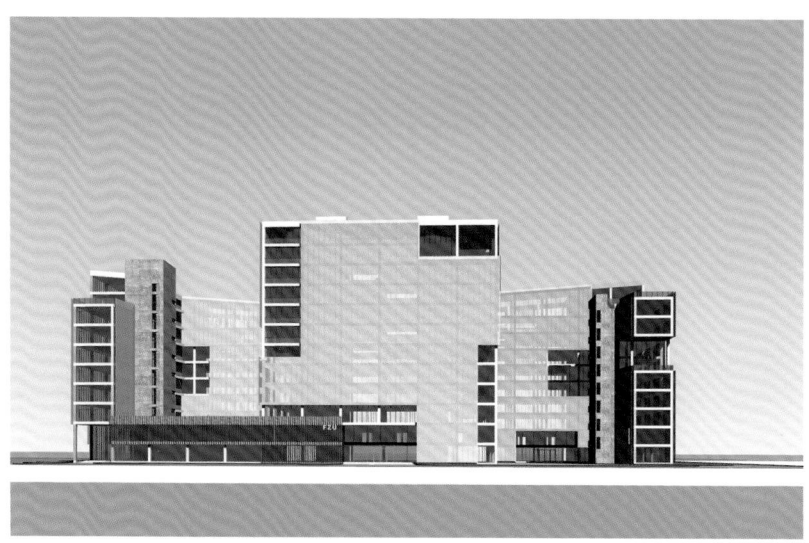
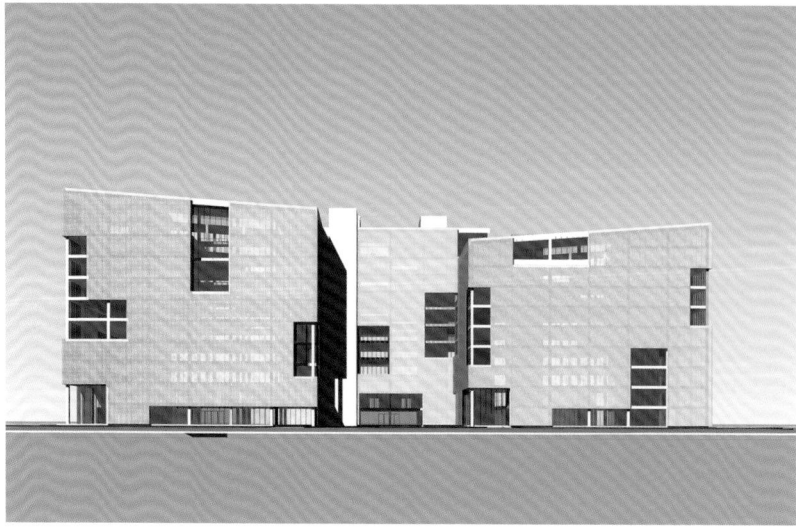

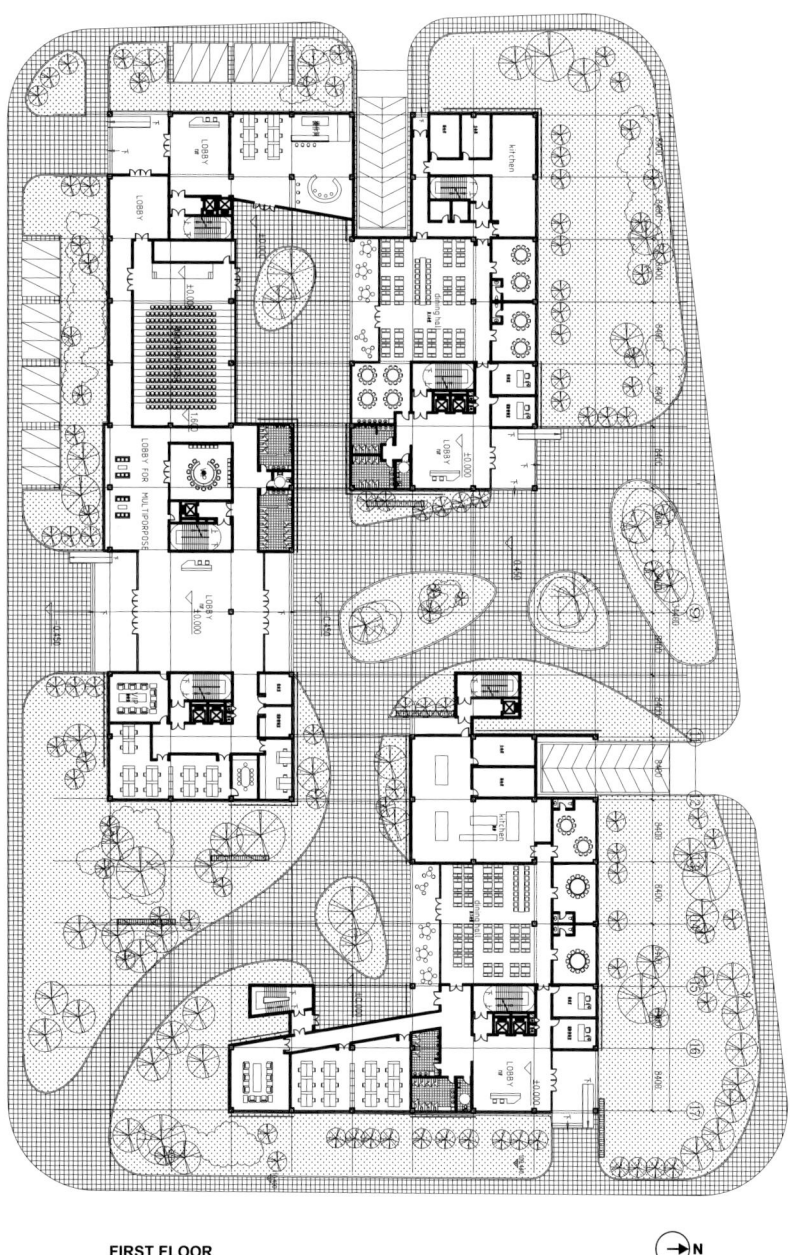

**FIRST FLOOR**

FUZHOU UNIVERSITY RESEARCH BUILDING

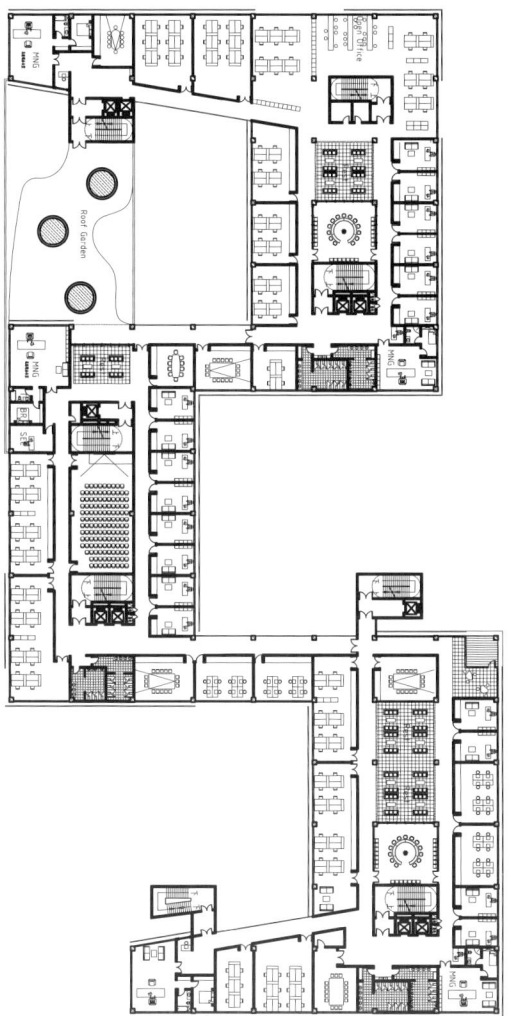

**THIRD FLOOR**